To Flo.

France 360°

photographed by **Franck Charel**

written by **Jean Taverne**

translated from the original French
by **Florence Brutton**

METRO BOOKS
NEW YORK

Introduction

France is a compendium of colors, her villages and towns each reflecting the tones of local materials: light or dark wood, ochre or yellow soil, granite, sandstone, limestone, slate. As if those villages and towns had literally sprung up out of the Earth.

For five years, Franck Charel has roamed across this vast palette, a unique cultural and geological color chart that extends from Alsace to the Basque Country and Flanders to Corsica. He has scaled the peaks and high vantage points that reveal the fabric of the landscapes, the spirit of the settlements and the intimacy of their existence. And he has always waited for the light, mistress of any work of art, be it photographic or otherwise.

The sky itself contributes its own special character. The sulfurous skies of Brittany, or the bottomless blue skies of the Midi; the pearly, lightly hazy skies of the Loire, or the big, bold clouds of the skies in the north and east. Being on the extreme edge of a continent, France has as much variety as confetti. It is as if all the skies on the planet were drawn here before scattering to the four corners of the globe.

And then there is mankind, slowly, patiently fashioning a rural and urban environment to suit his needs; draining his fields and hedges; planning a habitat designed for the climate, which is in places very harsh and in others quite mild; celebrating his faith in a firework display of cathedrals, churches and chapels. The men who in the course of the past thousand years have built the France we know have done so with a profound respect for her geography, her colors and her materials.

This book is a homage to those men.

Jean Taverne

S
Δ

Ouessant, Créac'h Lighthouse
Brittany
(previous pages)

A magical horizon: in the blink of an eye, the pale marble sea beyond these lichen-scarred rocks can turn into a ski-run. Ouessant is notorious for its sudden mists, murderous reefs and violent sea currents running at speeds over six mph. This is where the Drummond Castle came to grief in 1896 while on her maiden voyage. You can see why the French say 'Qui voit Ouessant, voit son sang' ('he who sees Ouessant, sees his own blood'). Winter storms apart, however, the temperatures in January and February are said to be the mildest in France…

Sheep breeding and seaweed, from which beer is made, are the main sources of income for Ouessant's tiny population – not counting tourism. At night, the beacons of the Créac'h lighthouse (visible for some 40 miles around) and the slightly less powerful Stiff lighthouse, designed by Vauban, sweep the seas to reduce the chance of another Drummond Castle disaster.

N

Ile lighthouse   E

The Pointe du Raz
Brittany

Not a tree or leaf in sight. Just a jumble of rocky ridges, the often-raging sea and the endless sky. A 'raz' is a sea channel with a violent current. This one, between the Ile de Sein and the mainland, is watched over by the Vieille lighthouse, sited out to sea as a warning sign. In the 1980s, the people of Plogoff successfully thwarted attempts to build a nuclear power station here – a place subsequently spoilt by souvenir stores and a huge black parking lot. Today things are back the way they should be. You have to walk to this dagger-like point that plunges into the sea before re-emerging a few nautical miles away as the Ile de Sein, surrounded by its murderous whirlpools. In fact, it's impossible to separate the Pointe du Raz from the hell that is the Baie des Trépassés where every November 2 the ghosts of those who perished in a shipwreck go searching for those they loved in life.

S

W

Portsall
Brittany

A tranquil port in the Abers with a mass of pictu- resque rocks in the distance – it was on these rocks at 10pm on a stormy night in March 1978 that a Liberian-registered supertanker finally broke in two after a day spent battling the elements. The Amoco Cadiz, owned by Standard Oil of Indiana subsidiary Amoco, some spewed 230,000 tons of crude oil into the ocean and created the biggest oil slick in recorded history.

Starting at Le Conquet, the slick smeared the wes- tern and northern shoreline of Finistère, eventually reaching the Côtes-d'Amor and extending as far as Bréhat, Paimpol and Saint-Brieuc. A five-year lawsuit brought by 76 Brittany communes and a variety of professional organizations forced the shipping company to pay out 32 million dollars in damages to France and the communes concerned. Nobody footed the bill for the environmental damage.

Despite a grueling clean-up operation, less than 10 percent of the crude oil was actually recovered. The rest, paradoxically, was 'digested' by nature, devoured by those otherwise undesirable marine bacteria that feed on agricultural phosphates and nitrates.

In the course of ten years, high levels of agricultural and industrial pesticides gave the beaches what they needed to clean themselves – not much of a consolation when you remember that these pesti- cides continue to suffocate marine flora and fauna, producing toxic algae that endanger crusta- ceans and abalone.

N

E

W
Λ

N
Λ

The Lighthouse of Pontusval, Brignogan
Brittany

'Heathen land, pagan land' said the Irish monks who brought Christianity to Brittany. The Pontusval coastline, bordered by miles of deserted dunes, was originally inhabited by 'natives' who were said to attach flaming torches to the horns of cows so as to lure lost ships on stormy nights. The hapless crew, thinking help was at hand, would make straight for the coast and run onto the rocks. Who knows whether or not this nasty reputation was deserved – but bad weather was obviously a boon for the impoverished seaweed gatherers of Pontusval. Why resort to trickery when shipwrecks were a regular natural occurrence along this jagged coastline with its hidden reefs? Looting stranded ships was a lot better than harvesting seaweed. Thankfully, times have changed. Brignogan these days is a seaside resort, founded in 1930, facing onto a circular, almost enclosed cove, 500 yards wide. At low tide the cove dries up, uncovering superb beaches strewn with huge, rounded rocks that resemble a herd of dinosaurs or a mysterious labyrinth. Passing a magnificent, tapering standing stone 24 feet high and topped with a cross – you reach the Lighthouse of Pontusval (above), a 54-foot high revolving beacon, positioned out to sea on a remote headland. An enchanted site.

E ▲   S ▲

W
▲

N
▲

The standing stones of Carnac
Brittany

Pope Cornely (St Cornelius), pursued all the way from Rome by pagan hordes, looked behind as he reached the shores of Armorica to see an army of soldiers heading his way. Legend has it that he turned them into stone, leaving behind some 3,000 standing stones that litter a two and a half mile area around Carnac. It's an attractive legend but these standing stones do in fact pre-date our pope by at least two thousand years... Archaeologists are still struggling to understand their significance. Some of the stones are just a few inches high but many stand more than seven feet tall and weigh hundreds of tons. Each had to be rolled on rounded logs down a man-made ramp, then planted in a deep hole and wedged. A project of such difficulty must have had religious meaning. Did these standing stones represent divinities as some experts believe? Were they worshipped as fertility symbols? Or – and this is another hypothesis – do they in fact form an immense stone calendar? Those who support this idea point out that on four dates – November 8, February 4, May 6 and August 8 – the rising sun is directly aligned with the stones. These dates also correspond to the natural cycle of death and re-birth: sowing, germination, flowering and harvest time. Whatever the case, the symbolism is terrific.

E
▲

S
▲

N
△

E
△

The Ploumanac'h Lighthouse
Britanny

These glowing boulders, within striking distance of Perros-Guirec, have that newly baked look of rocks that were blasted out of the Earth's surface only yesterday, having simmered gently for millions of years in deep underground furnaces. They are in fact just 150,000 years old – a mere trifle on the geological timescale... This is the famous rocky jumble of Ploumanac'h: bubbles of pink granitic magma speckled with mica that brings out their coarse-grained texture. A wildly untidy heap of boulders, cracked, split, worn away by sea and salt, eroded and pummeled by the incessant wind. The Maison du Littoral, near the lighthouse, recounts the monumental history of these granite colossi and how they were quarried in nearby La Clarté. From the Cross of Lorraine in Colombey-les-Deux-Eglises to the New York skyscrapers, the pink rocks of Ploumanac'h punctuate the skylines of the world.

S
↑

W
↑

The seaside resort of Veules-les Roses
Upper Normandy
(following pages)

The little wooded valley of Veules-les-Roses between Saint-Valery-en-Caux and Dieppe is so short that it barely manages to cut into the cliff to form a little harbor. But never mind: this former fishing and weaving village turned into an agreeable seaside resort with the arrival of the so-called 'pleasure trains' from Paris. Suddenly, wealthy city people and artists of all kinds could escape to a peaceful haven to sample the exceptional quality of the Normandy coastal light. So it was that Veules, like its neighbors, became a riot of gabled, gritstone villas: English-style cottages and traditional Swiss, Basque and Scandinavian chalets. A green and pleasant setting strewn with gardens and rockeries full of fake wooden handrails, fake half-timbering and outlandish roofs. The Normandy coast is a repertoire of the whimsical, the extravagant, the bizarre and the frankly screwy. Which is all to the good in a region where prudence counts for everything.

N
△

E
△

Etretat Cliffs
Upper Normandy
(previous pages)

Panning slowly from left to right, what hits the eye is the famous natural arch of Etretat alongside the colossal tooth of some mysterious marine monster. Framing them both are the cliffs of Amont and Aval, eroded and sculpted by the sea.

There is neither a harbor nor any beach to speak of in Etretat. Only a shoreline strand of pretty rounded pebbles. But this wide-open landscape with its pale-colored rocks is food for the imagination.

Maurice Leblanc imagined that the 858-foot Aiguille was hollow and turned it into a secret cavern for Arsène Lupin. It was from here that on May 8 1927 flyers Nungesser and Coli took off in their Oiseau Blanc to attempt the first ever Transatlantic flight. They also became the first men in history to enjoy an aerial view of these white cliffs, gothic arches and the needle-studded coastline. Moments later, the sea had swallowed them up for good.

S
∆

W
∆

Les Petites-Dalles
Upper Normandy

Out at sea is what looks like a catamaran with two cliffs for its floats. A dreamy vision, watched over by imposing houses and beach cabins that brighten the emptiness like streetlights. On the shore, a handful of earthlings seem oblivious of the lonely Moses-figure issuing from the waves (right). Strange indeed. Is he fishing for shrimps at low tide, or a holidaymaker from one of those big houses? We are on the Côte d'Albâtre (alabaster coast) in Normandy and this is the seaside resort of Les Petites-Dalles, perched at the tip of an avenue of beech trees on a strip of land in the Pays de Caux region. They say that the Austrian empress Sissi stayed in nearby Sassetot in 1975. Not surprising really.

S
Λ

Barfleur
Lower Normandy

In the Middle Ages, this charming little port with its jumble of boats perched on their keels along the shore was actually the main departure point for crossings from Lower Normandy to the British coastline. A bronze medallion at the entrance to the harbor marks the spot where William the Conqueror set sail in 1066 to recapture England. A century later, Richard the Lion Heart would also depart from Barfleur to be crowned across the Channel. It was also here in 1120 that the flower of Anglo-Norman nobility perished, among them William the Conqueror's two grandsons, in the tragic wreck of the Blanche-Nef. The little town was almost entirely demolished in the Anglo-French War and only really made a comeback in the 17th Century. The harbor we see today dates from the 1850s. Though nothing like as important as it used to be, if offers good lobster fishing and is becoming increasingly popular with yachting enthusiasts, French and English alike.

The marine cemetery adjoining the fortress-like church of Saint-Nicolas (in the center of the picture) is a reminder that this coast has a long history of shipwrecks. Which is why Barfleur takes pride in its highly efficient sea-rescue station, seen in the background on the right.

N

E

E ▲

S ▲

The Mont Saint-Michel
Lower Normandy

An invitation to poetry. The Mont Saint-Michel may look as inspiring as ever but it is actually in serious trouble. At the present rate of silting, this jewel of French architectural heritage will soon no longer be an island due to the endlessly encroaching mudflats.

In a bid to prevent such a betrayal of its eternal identity, the island is now undergoing a five-year 'course of treatment' (finishing in 2010). First comes the transfusion: unblocking the Couesnon Estuary (behind us, at the edges of the picture) by building an eight sluice-gate dam designed to flush the mud and silt back out to sea.

Next comes 'surgery': removing the hideous road/dyke and huge parking lot that contribute to the silting-up of the island and substituting a 'walkway' on stilts. The final stage is to provide enough parking for 4,000 vehicles, near the barracks, roughly one mile away and sufficiently far from the monastery not to spoil the view. A railway station is another possibility. Visitors to the monastery (around three million every year) will either have to walk there or take a scenic shuttle across the walkway. A worthwhile project, surely, to conserve the dignity of a quite exceptional place that has been classed a world heritage site by UNESCO. In Buddhist terms, this shoreline represents the immensity of the Universe. In Christian terms, it is the very quintessence of contemplation. For anyone, it is a transcendental place. If ever there were an emblematic religious spot, this must be it.

W

Tombelaine

N

E
S

Honfleur
Lower Normandy

You have to imagine the Quai Sainte-Catherine and its ancient houses with corbelled balconies back in the time of Boudin, Sisley, Courbet and other Monet-like painters who first marveled at the quality of the coastal light in Normandy – 'inventing', albeit unwittingly, what we now call Impressionism. They lodged at the Auberge Saint-Siméon, on the hill, which had the good taste to allow them as much credit as they needed and conserved all of

the sheets and scraps of paper that carried their rough sketches. Many are still displayed at the inn, now a very fashionable hotel, and at the museum, home of Boudin's fabulous pastel studies of skies. He and his friends would set up their easels just about anywhere, including right here on the Quai itself, surrounded by fishing nets and lobster pots, overlooking the old dock where the seagulls whirled around the returning trawlers.

This artistic tradition lives on today in the art galleries along the Quai, but the overall atmosphere has been sanitized by a string of pubs, brasseries, restaurants and souvenir shops. The place is as picturesque as ever but there are now more tourists and amateur photographers than painters. From October to April however, Honfleur is restored, if not to its former charm then at least to that simple beauty that suits it so well.

W

N

S
⋏

W
⋏

Deauville
Lower Normandy

Folded parasols in Deauville, on a deserted beach. Nothing but the slim, solitary shadows of banners at half-mast – splinters of color set against an almost impossibly blue sky. Silence reigns. These flagpoles would be as disconcerting to a visitor from outer space as the standing stones of Carnac are to us. But everything is about to change. This almost forlorn-looking desert will shortly be teeming with people. Families will take the beach by storm, opening out the parasols in a tightly packed bouquet. Famous people will leave their yachts to walk the famous promenade just long enough to see and be seen. People will do what they usually do on beaches. Kids will tickle bare feet, throw sand in the eyes of those who are trying to read, or build sand castles that the sea will wash away like a dream.

N
△

E
△

Mers-les-Bains
Picardy
(following pages)

An unusual 'behind the scenes' look at a collection of beach huts below a swank waterfront lined with orange, lemon and cherry-colored houses. Bathed in a soft light, it's that peaceful time of day when holiday-makers sip cocktails on a pebbly beach that glimmers in the setting sun. The former farming village of Mers-les-Bains owes its appeal to Le Tréport – just visible in the background (right) – one of the first fishing and commercial ports with a direct rail link to Paris. As the little city grew increasingly inundated by tourists, the waterfront above this deserted shoreline became home to a string of Parisian-owned follies, studded with towers, pinnacle turrets and loggias. Mers-les-Bains – too little known like so many resorts in Normandy and Picardy – is actually an astonishing repository of *belle époque* seaside architecture.

E

W
▲

S
⋀

W
⋀

The Vineyards near Cuis
Champagne-Ardennes
(previous pages)

Champagne: let the party begin! Looking down from Mount Sinaï on the Montagne de Reims, which peaks at just 925 feet, one is surprised at the relative modesty of the local villages. The world's most famous, expensive winegrowing region boasts few castles or manor-houses, only solid buildings with discretely flowered gardens that encroach as little as possible on the slopes. It is the wine, not the properties, that has style here.

And Cuis on the Côte des Blancs (planted with Chardonnay vines) is no exception. Every inch of land counts on this vast horizon. Unlike most other wines, the finest Champagne is often a blend of wines from different vineyards or years, based on one or all three of the approved cultivars: the Pinot Noir, Pinot Meunier and the Chardonnay. Skilled blending is what guarantees the consistent quality of Champagne year on year.

N
▲

E
▲

Saint-Valery-en-Somme
Picardy

At low tide, 'the sea goes out so far that it might never return' exclaimed Colette in *Les Vrilles de la Vigne.* Saint-Valery-en-Somme lies some seven and a half miles from this estuary, on the borders of the Somme Canal dug in 1827. Visible in the distance, it looks a proper little city with its cobbled streets in the upper part of town overlooking gray-blue, marshy immensities of sand. In the placid harbor waters, gently bobbing shrimpers and commercial fishing vessels wait for high tide when they and sailors from Crotoy, opposite, will make for the English Channel via the long navigation channel, up around the Marquenterre Bird Sanctuary (a refuge for migratory birds from March to October). In the area around Cape Hornu at the tip of the 'dead cliff', they will try for the sole and other flat fish that sell so well here in the winter off-season – washed down with a dry white wine in restaurants large and small.

E

S

The Valley of the Meuse
Champagne-Ardennes

These four jagged rocks crown a spur that overlooks the River Meuse near Monthermé. Vaguely resembling horsemen, they are known as the 'Quatre Fils Aymon' (the four sons of Aymon) after a famous epic poem that is partly set in this area. Sons of the Duke of Ardennes, the four brothers return to the Court of Charlemagne where Renaud, the hot-headed eldest son, smashes the head of one of the Emperor's nephews for having grievously offended him.

Charlemagne is furious and orders the brothers' immediate arrest. But they leap onto their trusty steed Bayard, a magic horse faster than the wind that whisks them off to the heart of a nearby secret forest where they shelter with their mother Audes and build a fortified castle. Charlemagne finds out, lays siege and takes the fortress thanks to a traitor who Renaud draws and quarters before escaping with the help of Aude, symbol of the Ardennes motherland. Renaud

eventually joins a crusade to deliver Jerusalem and dies a saintly death on his return. He personifies liberty, courage and loyalty, virtues he shares with Bayard the horse that, having been hurled into the Meuse by Charlemagne with a boulder around his neck, breaks free and flies off 'like a lark'. This legend that was so popular in its time would one day be described as 'entirely devoid of reality and riddled with fables (moral lessons) from beginning to end'.

W

N

N

E

Wissant, Côte d'Opale
Nord-Pas-de-Calais

Visible in the distance some three miles away are the milky white cliffs of Cap Blanc-Nez (literally, 'cape white nose') formed around 100 million years ago when the continent still lay under water. In the foreground is one of the almost lurid green blockhouses built by the thousand along the Côte d'Opale by young people in the 'Service du travail obligatoire' – the compulsory labor service run first by Fritz Todt, Hitler's Minister for Armaments,

then Albert Speer. Here we have two quite different images of this little corner of France that is described in Dante's *Divine Comedy* as the then-leading port of embarkation for England. That was before it sank into the sands. It was northern industrialist Emile Segard who in the early 20th Century revived Wissant and turned it into a seaside resort open to all – a concept that was entirely new at the time. Then, alas, came the bombard-

ments of World War II. Even they however could not alter the subtle luminosity of this aptly named 'opal' coastline.

S

W

W
▲

N
▲

The slag heaps of Loos-en-Goële, near Lens
Nord-Pas-de-Calais

This view of the slag heaps near Lens perfectly captures the atmosphere of the Artois coal-mining basin – a flat region strewn with mountains of scoria and mining villages composed of identical rows of miners' cottages and small gardens. The mining families who live there fought a century-long battle for a decent wage and a proper health-care system to address silicosis, the 'miner's disease' that decimated the men. The law they wanted was finally passed in 1946. Mining often passed from father to son – teenagers could apply to become apprentices after a five-week training period.

The first mine was discovered by accident in 1842, in nearby Oignies when they were looking for water but found coal instead. This was also where the last pit closed down in 1991. In the interval, this basin provided work for 250,000 people of which a quarter came from Poland. In the underground mining galleries, pit ponies hauled the ore in darkness and eventually went blind; the men often worked in galleries with less than three feet headroom. Disasters were common: the worst one, in Courrières near Lens in 1906, claimed 1,100 victims. The end of mining marked the end of an era and with it, a labor aristocracy. These days some of the slag heaps are planted with trees and used as playgrounds in summer and ski runs in winter...

E

S

W
N

The Pont-Neuf, Paris
Île-de-France

To understand this unusual photo of the Pont-Neuf in Paris: remember that the dome of the 'Institut' and the 'Hôtel des Monnaies' at each end are actually behind us. An equestrian statue of Henri IV dominates the romantic Square du Vert-Galant, at the tip of the Ile de la Cité. On its left is a famous store built on the site of the city's first public water fountain, the Samaritaine, installed in the reign of Henri IV.

On the opposite side, the exquisite Place Dauphine is set amid elegant private 17th and 18th Century houses. Construction of the Pont-Neuf started in 1578, in the thick of the French Wars of Religion. But money soon ran out and it was not completed until 1604. Free of the traditional shops, this bridge became a favorite haunt for Parisians with an unbeatable view of the city and the then incredibly busy River Seine.

E
▲

S
▲

The Grand Ballon de Guebwiller
Alsace
(following pages)

The Ballon d'Alsace Massif stands at the border of Alsace with Lorraine and Franch-Comté, overlooking the Territoire (department) de Belfort and particularly the famous Trouée de Belfort. The peak of the massif, however, lies some 12 miles to the northeast, near Guebwiller, location of the 4,656-foot Grand Ballon. To get to it, you must first pass through the woods and dark pine forests that carpet its flanks.

Then suddenly, you emerge onto broad, hummocky pasturelands where the view extends all the way to the Alps in the south and the Donon Pass in the north – a solitary pass at the heart of the Vosges Mountains. Surrounding it are the vast mountainous forests of Abreschviller, Saint-Quirin, Turquestein, the Val de Senones and Mount Donon, bordered to the east by the spectacular Valley of the Bruche that links up with Strasbourg in Saint-Dié.

E

E ⋏

S ⋏

The Vineyards of Kaysersberg
Alsace
(previous pages)

The banners of the feudal castle of Kaysersberg fly over an intriguing, fortified bridge across the River Weiss. Built of pink granite, the bridge is one of the high spots on the Alsace Wine Route, in an area renowned for its plantings of Sylvaner, Gewurztraminer, Tokay, Riesling, Pinot Noir and other varietals that produce these highly original and spicy wines. Alsace is a symphony of color. Kaysersberg and to the south and north, Ammerschwihr, Turckheim, Colmar, Riquewihr, Hunawihr and Ribeauvillé, form a ribbon of characteristic architecture: beavertail tiles tinted with reddish brown; façades in tones of cream, white and ochre; bright red geraniums; and the good-luck symbolism of the diagonal patterns traced by the walnut-stained half-timbering. Doorways feature the pink to purplish-blue Vosges sandstone that forms the foundations of the houses.

N

The Mont Sainte-Odile

Alsace

Here we are on the Mont Sainte-Odile, dominating the entire Alsace Plain from a height of 2,488 feet on a site that is honored as a historical mecca and a Holy Place *par excellence.*

Odile, patron saint of Alsace, was born in 660 AD, the blind daughter of an Alsatian duke who tried to stifle her at birth because of her disability. Saved by a servant, Odile then miraculously recovered her sight some years later on the very day she was christened.

The duke eventually repented and donated all his worldly goods to his daughter which she, being extremely pious, used to build a monastery on the flanks of this pink sandstone cliff. Traces of it are still visible today amid the ruins of a Celtic wall. Odile's remains were laid to rest in the Sainte Odile chapel, built in her honor in the 12th Century and frequently modified since that time. Near the eponymous abbey, the chapel welcomes pilgrims and visitors alike.

S ⋀   W ⋀

The Place Stanislas, Nancy
Lorraine

Rarely has a king ever received a greater tribute from his father-in-law than this royal square in Nancy, created entirely in his honor. The splendor of its design was the wonder of Europe. The king in question was Louis XV and his father-in-law was Stanislas Leszczynski, the dethroned king of Poland to whom Versailles, with Austria's agreement, entrusted independent Lorraine in the secret hope that it would quietly return to the bosom of France – a shrewd and perceptive calculation that came to pass in 1766. The square, seen here under white clouds against a blue sky, is now restored to its former grandeur, newly repaved with pink sandstone from the Vosges Mountains after serving as a parking lot until 1983. The triumphal arch is the focal point (even if it is set back from the rest of the square) dedicated to the 'victorious' and 'peaceful' sovereign. Framing it on either side are two classical palaces with wide vaulted openings. Symmetry reigns supreme here. The 'tumultuous wrought ironwork that festoons the gates' (Patrick Grainville) likewise frames the fountains, constructed in lead and decorated with mythological motifs. The geometry of the City Hall lends a subtle lightness to its 100-yard long façade. Everything is perfect. Could the golden section have inspired this square with the 'golden doors'? Thousands of men built it but just four shaped it, starting with Stanislas himself. Made Duke of Lorraine at the age of 61, he remained an exceptional patron for 30 years. It was he who discovered Emmanuel Héré de Cory, the visionary Nancy-born architect who in turn picked the sculptor Barthélémy Guibal to design the fountains, and the blacksmith Jean Lamour to work his genius with the wrought iron.

N
△

E
△

N
▲

E
▲

The Ballon d'Alsace
Lorraine

A paraglider launches off from the Ballon d'Alsace, punctuating the sky over the Swiss Alps that lie before him. But there is more than one 'Ballon' in the Vosges Mountains. The highest peak in this range is the Grand Ballon, some 12 miles to the northeast, which dominates the Guebwiller Forest from its 4,656-foot summit. The Ballon d'Alsace itself peaks at just 4,000 feet and lies at the southern tip of the Vosges, watching over the Trouée de Belfort plateau. The mountain occupies a particularly important strategic position at the border of Alsace with Lorraine and Franche-Comté. An equestrian statue of Joan of Arc dating from 1909 commemorates Alsace's historic attachment to France. Another monument, erected four years earlier, celebrates that hero of (more) modern times, racing cyclist René Pottier. First to make it to the summit of the Ballon in the 1905 Tour de France, Pottier is said to have raced up the five and a half miles of zigzags at the then (and now) breathtaking speed of 12 mph. The two semi-circles of the scenic map indicate a spectrum of viewpoints, from the sometimes misty Alsace Plain to the Donon Mountain and as far south as Mont Blanc. The immediate area offers some superb walking, with trails leading to the Cascade du Rummel or the Saut de la Truite (both waterfalls) and on the other side the small and charming Lake Alfeld. In winter when the undulating pastures at the summit are covered with snow, this is a prime venue for cross-country skiers.

S

W

W △

N △

The Loue River Springs
Franche-Comté

Looking out from the Rock of Hautepierre pictured here, it is easy to visualize the steep-sided limestone valley where, winter and summer alike, the River Loue gushes from a 60 foot-high cave. It then tumbles through the Jura canyons, creating a series of waterfalls as it carves its passage through the heart of the spectacular Franche-Comté landscape. Hurtling past forges, ancient mills and old bridges, castles, ruined abbeys and villages that cling to its sheer banks, it calms down considerably from Ornans onward, framed by wooden balconies that were immortalized by locally-born painter, Gustave Courbet. This is an area rich with beauty spots, such as the fabulous Miroir de Scey-en-Varais where the lake reflects the ruined feudal castle. Further on, the Loue laps over the foot of Cléron Castle before offering some idyllic fishing to the anglers of Port-Lesney. Its now-sedate waters bathe the intriguing site of Arc-et-Senans, designed by 18th Century architect Claude-Nicolas Ledoux as a Utopian example of an ideal city. From there, the Loue ambles in a series of lazy meanders to the Doubs.

E

S

Village of Hautepierre

E
△

S
△

Joux Castle
Franche-Comté

In 1795, when Haiti was ceded to France, the Haitian Toussaint Louverture was appointed a general. However, he revolted against Bonaparte's army and was locked up in the sinister feudal fort of Joux, which was restored in the 17th Century by Vauban. Now an armaments museum, the castle lies on the border with Switzerland, some two and a half miles from Pontarlier, a small and chilly city in the heart of the spectacular Jura gorges. From there the castle looks out over the Doubs Valley and the dramatic 'Cluse de Mijoux', a narrow gorge where the River Doubs leaps from one Jurassic fold to another, slicing its way through 654-foot high limestone cliffs. A 'cluse' is a deep gorge characterized by steep scarps (a 'reculée' is a blind valley with a creek emerging at its head).

W
∆

N
∆

The Rock of Solutré
Burgundy
(following pages)

The jagged outline of the Rock of Solutré adds vibrancy to the tranquil lines of the vineyards of Mâcon, lit from behind by the morning sun. The rock's telltale shadow bears witness to a landform that starts as a gentle hill then rises abruptly to more than 1,600 feet. In his youth, François Mitterand used to climb the rock every Whit Monday, a tradition that subsequently turned into a pilgrimage. Some 20,000 years ago now, the rock and its surroundings were occupied by Paleolithic hunters who left behind a pile of animal bones several yards thick (horses, bison, aurochs and even mammoths) that litters a one-hectare area at the foot of the cliff. The lives of those distant ancestors are described in a great underground museum at the foot of the rock.

W

N

W
▲

N ⋀   E ⋀

Village of Meursault

The Puy Mary
Auvergne
(previous pages)

A cluster of mountains beneath a sky of melted gold. At its heart is the immense cone of the Puy Mary (5,843 feet), a fabulous viewpoint deep within the spectacular scenery of the Cantal Massifs.

The flanks of the 'puy' (mountain) are lined with basalt, planezes (grassy, triangular plateaus) and star-shaped valleys. Framing the mountain are two of the loveliest villages in France: Murat and especially Salers whose ancient lava houses with

their 'lauze' roofs (a kind of scalloped, schist tile) occupy a superb site overlooking the Maronne Valley. The mountain towers over the torrents that carve out the canyons in the valleys of Falgoux, La Maronne and La Jordanne, looking down on abandoned 'burons' once used to make cheese at high altitude. The picturesque villages of Cantal, lower down, are studded with farms and sheepfolds.

S ⋏   W ⋏

The vineyards around Meursault
Burgundy

The little town of Beaune with its glazed-tile roofs is the hub of the aptly named 'Côte d'Or' ('golden slope'), one of the showpieces at the heart of Burgundy. Nestling alongside are other Burgundian masterpieces such as Vézelay, Autun and Cluny. To the north reigns the Côte de Nuits, home of the delectable-sounding Pinot Noir vineyards of Gevrey-Chambertin, Romanée, Nuits-Saint-Georges and Pommard.

To the south of Beaune lies a positive kingdom of white wines that starts in Meursault, its plain visible here at the foot of slopes planted to the Chardonnay. From Tokyo to New York, every sommelier has surely heard of Saint-Romain, Corton-Charlemagne or the eight-hectare vineyard of Montrachet – a wine to be drunk on bended knee, said Alexandre Dumas.

N
▲

E
▲

La Rochepot Castle
Burgundy

An emblematic image of Burgundy: the multi-colored, glazed rooftops of La Rochepot Castle glimpsed through a sea of vines in a small, lush green valley. Its history would be defined by two families who lived several centuries apart.

The first was the Pot family. Régnier Pot, future knight of the Golden Fleece, acquired the castle in 1403. More important however is his grandson, Philippe, whose variable allegiances are a diplo-

mat's delight. He would slip smoothly from the service of first his godfather Philippe Le Bon (Philippe the Good) to his son Charles le Téméraire (Charles the Bold) then to their worst enemy Louis XI who annexed Burgundy for France in 1477.

In the French Revolution, the castle itself became a source of stone but the 12th Century chapel was curiously spared. Enter the Carnot family in 1893 when a local girl – wife of French President Sadi

Carnot, son of the revolutionary general and nephew of the celebrated physicist – purchased the castle as a gift for her son, Colonel Hippolyte Sadi Carnot. He then spent the next 30 years carefully restoring the castle, complete with 12-foot thick walls, a double drawbridge, a two-story guardroom with room to accommodate the entire village in wartime, a covered way and a 235-foot well dug out of the rock by hand in 1228. The

present-day owner is Sylvie Carnot, a descendant of the assassinated President.

S

W

W

⋀

N

⋀

Clermont-Ferrand

The Puy de Dôme
Auvergne

As the setting sun sinks behind the fading outline of the Chaîne des Puys, its dying rays glimmer across the suburbs of Clermont-Ferrand.

The 4,790-foot Puy de Dôme is the highest peak in this immense, pyramid-shaped range. It is also specially venerated for a victory in 52 BC, at the hill fort of Gergovie just a stone's throw away, where Vercingétorix and his army beat off an assault by Caesar's legions. From the top of the Puy, there is a fabulous, balcony-like view of some 60 craters that extend from north to south. Now long extinct, some 6,000 years ago they spewed out flows of lava that covered this area for miles around.

The lava that erupted from the Puy de Dôme was light and viscous and solidified almost instantly, forming the dome that we see today (hence its local name of 'domite'). These effects are simulated at the recently built 'Vulcania' Museum ('Musée des Volcans d'Auvergne') where visitors can relive the drama that created one of France's most remarkable regions.

In summer the summit is accessible by car and the crowds can be discouraging. For those who value their tranquility, the Grand Sarcouy to the north is easily reachable on foot. The path goes by way of a permeable rock that once served as a sarcophagus in which bodies were mummified...The view from the top is as magical as the view from the Puy de Dôme, opposite – and remains deliciously undisturbed.

E

S

W
⋏

N
⋏

The Puy de Lassolas
and the Puy de La Vache
Auvergne

Seen from an airplane on a clear day, the Chaîne des Puys range offers a vivid lesson in geology and geography. This is a very young mountain range, formed just 100,000 years ago when *Homo sapiens* first appeared. The pure, clean outlines of the volcanoes with their closed or sunken craters form a dead straight line that runs more or less north-south for more than 12 miles. A fascinating land-scape of barren, deserted expanses. Alexandre

Vialatte used to say it was 'like looking at a piece of the moon' and considered himself marked for life by his excursions into this 'land of volcanoes'. The Puy de Dôme is plainly visible in this picture; to the south of it lie the 'puys' (mountains) of Lassolas (left) and La Vache (right). Among the most famous of sunken volcanoes, they are thought to have disgorged successive waves of lava as part of a single, stupendous eruption that lasted

several days, if not weeks or months. Experts believe that cinders and lava must have erupted at the same time. As the cinders accumulated on the dense, molten lava flows, part of the cone broke away, leaving the variable-length crescent-shaped craters that we see today. These are steep-sided volcanoes, covered with pozzolana that retains its reddish tint because it was still hot when it landed. A trek along these twin mountains, under moving

skies as beautiful as those pictured here, offers some sublime views over the range as a whole.

E

S

W
N

N

The Puy de Sancy
Auvergne

Still in the Auvergne, we are now in the Dore Mountains, immediately south of the Dôme Mountains, at the heart of the regional park. Out of the bowels of the volcano rises the Puy de Sancy, some 2.5 miles from the Mont Dore spa and more than 6,000 feet high. It dominates the Massif Central and the amphitheatre where the River Dordogne rises. This is a land of planezes, wide, naked grasslands that shield the land against new eruptions – a land tinged with 'dreamy melancholy' ' (George Sand) and carpeted with daffodils, narcissi and gentian in spring and early summer. A world of summer pastures dotted with cattle and sheep. Saint-Nectaire was once produced here at altitude. The livestock today is fattened by salaried shepherds. A cable car up the mountain carries hikers, skiers and all those who seek pure air and aerial views that extend to infinity.

S

E

S

Batz-sur-Mer
Pays de la Loire
(following pages)

This is the wild coastline of Batz-sur-Mer, capital of the salt marshes of La Brière. Come December, it is pummeled by violent storms. The wind howls, the sky rips apart and an apocalyptic light descends on the village. But the rainbow is never very far away. Immediately beyond the coast and its rows of houses, you have the treeless checkerboard of the salt marshes. Sheltered from the wind, they still produce salt but the reward today is relatively poor for the salt workers of Batz. Gradually the town became overshadowed by the neighboring port of Le Croisic that rapidly turned to fishing and canning, which was then in its infancy, and particularly balneotherapy. Batz, just over six miles from Guérande, nevertheless remains a fine gateway to the unique regional park of La Brière, a land of canals, marshes, peat and islands – Fédrun, Mazin and Errand – scattered with charming white hamlets.

E ▲   S ▲

Oléron Island
Poitou-Charentes
(previous pages)

It would be hard to improve on the simple beauty of these oystermen's huts under luminous skies, set in the middle of the old salt marshes facing the Fouras Coast – the perfect evocation of a human-scale industry, untouched by the supercharged atmosphere of the holiday season. The island's population has doubled in the past half century. Holiday homes are partly responsible but so too are the oysters of Marennes-Oléron that make a significant contribution to the island's economy. Fort Boyard, a castle built in the reigns of the two Napoleons, is clearly visible from Oléron. The island is traditionally known for its mimosa, oysters and vines, but we might also mention the curious fishing weirs that are still visible on the northern side: low, very thick stone walls built on the shoreline, designed to trap fish as the tide retreated.

W
△

N
△

Parcé-sur-Sarthe
Pays de la Loire

This is the kingdom of that 'gentle France' – a serene, peaceful landscape of well-tamed rivers and villages dotted with steeples, manor-houses and mills, ancient houses polished by time... a France made for a life of tranquil routine and simple pleasures like angling. The river is watched over by the strongholds of Ravadun and Pêcheseul, and Parcé-sur-Sarthe would not have prospered without them.

In the late 18th Century, Parcé was the site of Claude Chappe's first experiments with aerial telegraphy – an early step towards modern telephony. But Parce's particular source of pride and joy is a much more recent historical connection. It was here, in the millhouse at Ignères, that the famous southern French writer Marcel Pagnol retired in the 1970s.

W
▲

N
▲

Aiguillon-sur-Mer
Pays de la Loire

A regiment of oak pilings stands to attention – moorings for boats and habitats for mussels. But for how much longer? Aiguillon Bay is gradually drying up, as the land in these parts encroaches inexorably on the sea.

This charming harbor lies tucked away in a narrow estuary facing Arçay Point. A refuge for large migratory birds, it was formed some 1,000 years ago at about the same time as the neighboring Marais-Poitevin. In the time of Carolingian rule, the sea still extended from Luçon in the north to Esnandes in the south and inland to Marans and beyond. Behind Aiguillon Bay, the network of canals and inlets of the Marais tell the story of a Dutch-style battle to reclaim land and turn it into fertile polders. In former times, cows in the Marais were taken to pasture on small boats. Today all that remains of the immense gulf that once reached all the way to Niort is this tranquil bay full of plankton and its little, unpretentious harbor with its oyster and mussel beds. That peaceful seaside location is doomed to disappear just as it did in Brouage farther south. Once an important military port to rival La Rochelle, Brouage these days sits stranded one and a half miles inland, its ten hectares of pink and white ramparts looking out on a damp landscape criss-crossed with salt marshes ...

E

S

N

E

La Tremblade, in the oyster farming basin of Marennes
Poitou-Charentes

Oyster baskets, crushed shells and vagabond clouds: this is the Seudre fairway, home to flat-bottomed barges and oystermen's cabins. We are in La Tremblade, heart of the Marennes Basin where the salt marshes have been transformed into 3,000 hectares of oyster beds. This is France's leading oyster-producing region, with some 2,000 producers and an exceptionally favorable environment, protected from the wind and enriched by fresh water that reduces salt content. At around five years of age, the oysters are fattened-up in shallow, mineral-rich pools known as 'claires' where they absorb a scented pigment called 'marennine'. Produced by the marine microalgae, 'blue navicula', it is this that gives oysters their greenish hue and characteristic taste of the sea. So-called 'fines de claires' oysters spend two months in these basins, at a density of around 20 oysters to the square meter; 'spéciales' oysters remain there for three times as long (six months) but with four times as much space. At the end of that time, the oysters must purge themselves of any remaining silt and sand, retaining just enough of their liquid to reach the market stalls alive. Enjoy! Whether they suffer or not is a matter for your conscience ...

S
W

N

E

Chenonceaux Castle
Centre

Building a castle on a bridge across a river is just about every child's dream. It was Diane de Poitiers in the 16th Century who commissioned the construction of an immense terrace across the River Cher, built on the foundations of an ancient mill and supported by five arches with sharp angles to part the current. When she ran short of money, her lover the King of France, Henri II, raised a tax on church bells to fund the works. The ever-generous bishops of Tours then showered her with all manner of lilies, roses, pear, plum and mulberry trees that she arranged at the water's edge around eight large triangles of greenery planted with trimmed yew trees, hibiscus bushes, laurels, box ...

Alas, when Henri II died in 1559, the castle passed to Diane's rival: none other than Catherine of Médicis, Queen of France. It was she who ordered the construction of the 180-foot long, two-story galleries on the bridge that were reserved for grand receptions. To the west, their huge bay windows overlook the peaceful, bucolic waters of the Cher and the garden designed by the queen to the right of the keep. Its layout, pictured here, remains largely unchanged: a central, circular pool surrounded by eight areas of lawn planted with rose bushes and flowerbeds. The flowers come from the gardens, near the old farm: 80,000 plants each year, and that's not counting all the cut flowers that go to make the 20 huge and spectacular bouquets, replenished twice weekly, on show inside the castle.

S
▲

W
▲

W
▲

N
▲

Amboise Castle
Centre

This castle with its two colossal towers overlooks the banks of the nonchalant Loire and the charming little city of Amboise. It was once home to two outstanding kings of France: Charles VIII and François I, who completed the Renaissance wing facing us here. François, crowned king in 1515 at the age of 21, persuaded Leonardo da Vinci to settle in Amboise, and they soon became firm friends. The young king would often visit the old man, walking down nearly half a mile of underground tunnel that linked the castle to the manor. Together they dreamed up a huge number of projects, one of which at least did eventually materialize: the famous twin spiral staircase of Chambord. Sadly, Leonardo died within three years and his remains are said to have been laid to rest in the chapel of Saint-Hubert. It is seen here on the right of Amboise Castle and is therefore – thanks to panoramic photography – actually behind us.

E
⋏

S
⋏

The Great Dune of Pyla
Aquitaine
(following pages)

A pocket-sized Sahara, set against a background of mirages and improbable clouds – what exactly are we looking at here? Pines form a ring at each end. In between, there are twin mounds of ochre sand with smooth, windswept surfaces here and there. Such is the magic of a panoramic 360-degree shot that can create a purely imaginary view of the Great Dune of Pyla. We are at the far west of Bordeaux, at the tip of the Arcachon Basin, over-looking the Arguin Bird Sanctuary. 'Pila' is the ancient French word for 'pile', referring to this huge mass of moving sand that formed as a dune in the 18th Century and now measures more than 370 feet in height, nearly two miles long and 1,635 feet wide. Deserted in the off-season, this is the perfect place to look out onto the narrow Cape Ferret channel (Les Passes) and its strip of land that is shaped like an open beak.

E

S

N

E

Lescun
Aquitaine
(previous pages)

Lescun is a little known place in the Béarn – the last stop on the road that zig-zags up to it from the Aspe Valley. But the view is to die for: a white village studded with very old houses where animals were once kept on the ground floor; and all around, one of the finest cirques in the Pyrenees. Streaming out of those distant mountain walls are the 'gaves' (torrents) of Lescun and Lauga that join up in Lescun from whence they hurtle toward Aspe. There are no tourists here, only nature lovers, lodging in the village itself or just above it in the Labérouat mountain refuge – an ideal summer departure point for the 3,000-foot climb up to the Pic d'Anie (8,188 feet), the Table des Trois Rois and the Pic d'Ansabère (7,772 feet). From there, you get a bird's-eye view of Spain.

S

W

The Mont Gargan
Limousin

Mount Gargan (2,390 feet) stands between Limoges and the Millevaches plateau. From here you get a breathtaking view of the mountains of the Limousin, of Ambazac, Les Monédières and, weather permitting, the Puy de Sancy. This region was the site of violent confrontations between the French Resistance and the German army in the Second World War – witness the church pictured here, burned down by the Germans. To the left of it, an engraved rock commemorates the events of July 18-24 1944 when FTP forces under Lieutenant-Colonel Guingouin fought off a German combat unit. Some 12 miles to the north, the Eymoutiers Art Center features a large canvas titled 'Le Cyclope', by local artist Paul Rebeyrolle (1926- 2005). The work is a homage to Guingouin who was a primary school teacher in Saint-Gilles-les-Forêts, at the foot of Mount Gargan, before retiring nearby.

W
△

N
△

Saint Emilion
Aquitaine

Everyone – meaning the whole world – knows the wines of Saint Emilion, but not necessarily the place itself, which is one of the most outstanding and unusual in France. The core of this small town is in fact an extraordinary troglodytic network developed in the 8th Century by the Breton monk Emilion, a travelling confessor and specialist in miracles. What was hewn out of the rock here by Emilion and his followers is the most enormous underground church in Europe, with three naves, catacombs and a hermitage where all the 'furniture' is cut directly into the rock. This extraordinary ensemble sits at the heart of Saint Emilion, alongside the collegiate church – built above the ground – with its tall bell-tower (photo) and its cloister, dating from the 12th-14th Centuries. Caught in the war between France and England, the little city surrounded itself with ramparts and its inhabitants used to take refuge in the king's castle. This photo is taken from the terrace of the castle's mighty keep – the place where ever year in mid-September the members of the 'Jurade' (wine brotherhood originally founded in 1199) appear in their formal regalia to proclaim the official start of the harvests in Saint Emilion's 12 Premiers Grands Crus and its 60 or so Grands Crus.

E

S

W
△

N
△

Biarritz
Aquitaine

The little whaling port of Biarritz, sitting askew on 'grass and heather-covered hilltops', was such a favorite with Victor Hugo that he worried it might become fashionable. 'People are already coming here from Madrid', he remarked in 1843. They were also pretty quick to arrive from Paris, taking their lead from 'Napoléon le Petit' and his wife Eugénie who transformed Biarritz into a seaside resort that has never gone out of fashion. Witness the sheer

number of villas – cubic, Anglo-Norman, neo-medieval, neo-Basques – complete with belvederes, caryatids, stained-glass windows, watchtowers, terraces, tangled balconies, ceramic walls, fake half-timbering ... The past half century looks pretty drab compared with all these joyful eccentricities.

This is where the lower Atlantic coast and its dunes give way to the cliffs and rocks of a stunningly rugged coastline. The city's famous boule-

vards run along the cliffs, lined with gardens full of flowers, overlooking the magnificent Grande Plage bordered by the casino (left), and the little port below the church (right).

But the most impressive and occasionally terri-fying view is from the 180-foot high Côte des Basques, immediately to the south, where the waves in the equinoctial periods can reach heights of more than 60 feet. Which is why these flanks of

chalky sandstone need continuous reinforcement against the colossal power of the ocean. Today however the sea is like a millpond and we can enjoy the setting sun.

E

S

W
△

N
△

Ciboure and the Fort de Socoa
Aquitaine

Just imagine the battering-ram power of an enraged sea hurling a 40-ton block of rock right over this jetty that leads to the Fort de Socoa. Imagine the same thing back in the 'thirties, powerful enough to uproot more than 180 feet of sea wall – that's 10,000 tons – and push it back several yards. Now picture that actually happening, in the area directly ahead of us, at the back of the picture, behind the whitish boundary of Saint-Jean-de-

Luz. Under a fine summer sky, one would never guess the incredibly erosive force of the Atlantic that forever ravages this coast at the foot of the Pyrenees. The rock is flysch, or Bidache limestone, a thick but not very solid formation that folds, tears and twists - as you can easily see here, below the military fort that was built in the reign of Louis XIII to protect the coast against repeated Spanish incursions. In the foreground is the man-made

dock from which cod fishermen and whalers used to leave for Quebec. At the exit to the port, they would pass the crumpled flysch rocks of the Pointe Sainte-Barbe that closes the Bay of Ciboure, then head out to sea, wide of the Rhune Mountain with its little rack-and-pinion train that opens up a panorama of the Basque country as it climbs. And with that, the fishermen would disappear for long months.

But not anymore: these days the last remaining fishermen catch sardines and look forward to the tuna season.

E

La Rhune Mountain

S

W

N

Albi
Midi-Pyrénées

View of the Tarn, the Pont-Vieux and a section of the right bank showing the formal gardens of Berbie Palace in the center of Albi. The walkway along the river was built on the former curtain walls of the palace that was designed as an episcopal citadel in 1240. The gallery pictured here, with its large supporting arch, was built much later to give a more human face to this deliberately very austere ensemble. Similarly austere is the neigh-boring cathedral of Sainte-Cécile, a masterpiece of southern Gothic architecture, but also a religious fortress with a mighty bell tower/keep. In the thick of the Catharist 'heresy', the bishops of Albi expressed their power through monuments in a sober architectural style, based on austere building materials (brick). Berbie Palace today is an elegant museum that includes works by locally-born artist, Toulouse-Lautrec.

S
Λ

The Pic du Midi d'Ossau
Midi-Pyrénées
(following pages)

Late May and the last névés linger on the banks of little Lake Ayous in the Pyrenees National Park. In the background, almost center, is the 9,430-foot Pic du Midi d'Ossau, a molar-shaped mass of rock close to the Somport and Pourtalet mountain passes. Straddling the Franco-Spanish border, it commands an interesting view of the Ossau Valley. For centuries, the high pasturelands used for seasonal grazing were collectively owned so as to safeguard the valley's prosperity. Other sources of livelihood were leather, wood and marble, which served to make window surrounds for churches and other buildings. Roadside villages such as Buzy, Izeste and Louvie-Juzon testify to a region of plenty: imposing slate-roofed houses with basket-handle arches over huge doorways, and manor houses, castles and churches emblazoned with two typical regional symbols, the cow of Béarn and the bear of Ossau.

S
▲

E
Λ

S
Λ

Grande Cascade waterfall

The Pic de Tentes
Midi-Pyrénées
(previous pages)

There is a very pretty road up to the Pic de Tentes mountain pass. Nearby is the Cirque de Gavarnie, a landform so astonishing that Victor Hugo apparently lost all sense of proportion ('that high and mighty boulevard that bars the continent from one sea to another'). The Pic de Tentes itself overlooks the Pic des Sarradets and the Brèche (breccia) de Roland, at the foot of the Taillon Mountain (right) that peaks at more than 10,000 feet. This is where the Franks fought the Moors. Roland, attacked from the rear, sounded his hunting horn to alert Charlemagne up ahead but to no avail. On the point of defeat, Roland preferred to shatter his sword on a rock rather than surrender it to the enemy, striking a mighty blow that opened up a gash 260 feet deep by 163 feet wide...

W
▲

N
▲

The Cirque de Gavarnie
Midi-Pyrénées

At the level where Franck Charel (the photographer) is standing, the base of the Cirque de Gavarnie measures just 2,616 feet across. Towering over it, however, are waterfalls and huge terraces that bring its total circumference to more than nine miles. This place streams with water summer and winter alike. In summer the highest waterfall (1,379 feet) makes a noise like thunder. In winter it glitters with silent stalactites that hang from the

rock in the freezing air. At their highest, facing the Grand Astazou, these mountainous walls reach more than 9,800 feet. Up there, lost in blue, you see the vestiges of the colossal glacier that originally carved out this valley. Strange as it may seem, these various cirques with their gigantic walls, from Troumouse to the Pic de Tentes, have always served as thoroughfares and meeting places. But their most legendary historical connection is of

course with Charlemagne's armies and the valiant Roland, reputed author of the celebrated breccia just visible here.

S
▲
Pic du Tourmalet

W
▲

Pic du Tourmalet

The Pic du Midi de Bigorre
Midi-Pyrénées

The 9,368-foot Pic du Midi de Bigorre commands a view of the Pyrenees for more than 60 miles around. On a clear day, the mountain itself is visible from Toulouse. A scenic map at the summit pinpoints views in every direction, starting with the Le Tourmalet Mountain, seen here in the foreground. When Madame de Maintenon visited the area in the 17th Century to 'take the waters' she found it quite enough to climb the 6,929-foot pass... in a sedan chair! In the

19th Century, the local intelligentsia picked the Pic du Midi as a particularly good place to study the stars, and set up an observatory here. The materials were carried up on the backs of men and mules, and a handful of astrophysicists settled here in 1881.
Living conditions were particularly harsh and communications difficult: the winds often blow at close to 125 mph and there is snow and ice for seven months of the year.

The building of the cable car in the 'fifties simplified things enormously. Some thirty researchers took turns at the summit, which today boasts the biggest telescope in France (6.5 feet in diameter) housed in a vast dome. Some of the best photos of the lunar surface have been taken from here, working in collaboration with Nasa. This is also the site of a 343-foot high antenna that provides radio and television coverage across one quarter of France.

N

E

E △   S △

The Pic de Néouvielle
Midi-Pyrénées

Behind us, the Pyrenees National Park and its Spanish equivalent, the Ordesa Park. In front, névés (a mass of porous ice), sheets of ice, lakes cupped in rocky hollows and the Pic de Néouvielle rising to 10,107 feet under a sky brushed with clouds. Surrounded by mountain pines, the route climbs to more than 6,867 feet, as far as Lakes Aumar and Aubert at the base of this formidable mountain – a three-hour journey on foot. A proportion of the water from these lakes supplies the gravity-arch dam of nearby Cap-de-Long, flowing via a four-mile tunnel carved out of granite with a fall of 4,087 feet. The 327-foot high dam is one of the jewels of the Pyrenees, with a capacity of 2,365 million cubic feet of water destined for the impressive Pragnères power station in the valley of the Gave (torrent) de Gavarnie. Definitely worth a visit. The granite massif of Néouvielle is so far relatively free of visitors. A listed nature reserve, strewn with peat bogs and lakes bordered by rare flora, it makes an ideal place for superb springtime rambles, when the rhododendrons are flowering.

If you go quietly, you might see chamois bounding gracefully from rock to rock, or watch Eurasian griffon vultures in flight, looking for prey. What you will not see is a bear, which remains as elusive as it is legendary in these parts.

Pic de Néouvielle

W

N

W

N

Perpignan

The Pic du Canigou
Languedoc-Roussillon

The Tramontane wind has purified the air. From the top of Mount Canigou, 9,103 feet up, a climber admires the evening light illuminating the flat lands of Perpignan and the blue of the Golfe du Lion, bordered by a pale strip between Collioure and Argelès.

This extraordinary viewpoint sits atop a rocky massif that is decorated from the bottom up with red pomegranate flowers set against a background of subtle greens. Figs, oaks, olives, firs, beech and ash each add their touch, framed by bright green cactus down in the valleys and the freshness of the high mountain pasture above. At the feet of the massif are the abbeys of Saint-Michel-de-Cuxa and Saint-Martin-du-Canigou, two of the first great Romanesque abbeys built by the monks one thousand years ago. We will never know whether they saw this peak as a sacred mountain but the fact remains that the surrounding villages all followed suit, each building churches more meditative than the last. Saint-Michel-de-Cuxa was built in the fine pink marble of Villefranche-de-Confluent, some six miles away, but time took its toll and parts of the cloister collapsed. The stones were then bought and carefully numbered by certain wealthy, heritage-loving Americans who shipped them home on an extraordinary convoy. Perfectly reconstructed, the superb cloister of Saint-Michel is today the jewel of one of New York's most unlikely museums – the Museum of Cloisters. You gotta hand it to those Americans ...

E
△

S
△

N
Δ

E
Δ

The Corniche des Cévennes
Languedoc-Roussillon

Even this bold light cannot redeem the starkly arid nature of this plateau of alternating pinewoods, agricultural clearings, moors and rocky banks, extending along a ridge above the Française Valley and running all the way to Barre-des-Cévennes – impoverished lands as poor as the people who work them.

Many were Protestants, so poor that they were known as 'camisards', from 'camiso', meaning 'shirtless' in southern French dialect. In 1685 they rebelled after being denied freedom of worship by the revocation of the Edict of Nantes. Louis XIV retaliated by turning this broad shepherds' track into a cliff road, then sending in the troops. Every September, the Mas-Soubeyran, a mecca of French Protestantism, welcomes thousands of 'pilgrims' who come to remember the victims of a century of religious intolerance.

S
▲

W
▲

Collioure
Languedoc-Roussillon
(following pages)

A tranquil May morning in Collioure. This ancient fortified town dominated by the square keep of the former royal castle has looked the same for 100 years. Ever since Matisse stepped down from the Paris train in the spring of 1905 and lodged at the Auberge de Rosette. At age 35, he had already made a name for himself but he felt a pressing need for change. Here he was, on his own, with just one simple rule: 'to make the colors sing'. Overcome with enthusiasm, he asked his friends to come and join him. Derain, 10 years Matisse's junior, did so and fell in love with Collioure. Between them, Matisse and Derain painted some 50 canvasses and as many watercolors in the course of a single summer – a blaze of luminous yellows, mossy greens and deep blues. Breaking with convention, they 'invented' a style based on bold brushstrokes and stark use of paint that we would later call 'Fauvism'.

W
▲

W

W
Λ

Cape Croisette
Provence-Alpes-Côte d'Azur
(previous pages)

Who would think it? We are in fact at the southern gateway to Marseilles, tucked at the back of Cape Canaille whose sheer limestone cliffs drop straight down to the sea. From here the famous 'calanques' (creeks) extend for some 12 miles all the way to Cassis. Dominating Cape Croisette is Marseilleveyre Mountain, once carpeted with holm oaks and Aleppo pines. This impressive cape looks out to the jagged rocks of Maïre Island that still bears the traces of a maritime customs post. This is the most western island in a small archipelago that is a haven for wild birds, fishermen and divers who 'explore' the dozens of shipwrecks. The coast here is notoriously dangerous in bad weather – witness the cross seen here in the foreground. In days gone by, modest Marseilles families built cottages in the surrounding calanques and families still come here on Sundays to enjoy precious moments within striking distance of the big city.

E
Λ

S
Λ

The Tarn Gorge
Languedoc-Roussillon

This view from the Méjean 'causse' shows La Malène, a deep and narrow gash between the limestone plateaus of Méjean and Sauveterre, deep in the Tarn Gorge. Immediately next to La Malène is an even more spectacular sight that has to be seen from the river: the smooth, sheer, giddy walls of the Détroits (straits), amid the myriad rocks and promontories of the Cirque des Baumes. Right at the top, a path weaves between natural towers, needles and cop-pices toward Point Sublime that offers sensational views on all sides. These 30 odd miles of gorges and canyons between Espinasse and Le Rozier are best seen in early spring when flowers carpet the 'causses' and the cherry orchards blossom in the Ispagnac Valley. Castles and villages cling to the flanks of the Méjean Causse, all the way to the little city of Sainte-Enimie where the streets are paved with Tarn pebbles.

S
▲

E
▲

S
▲

Sénanque Abbey
Provence-Alpes-Côte d'Azur

Together with Le Thoronet and Silvacane, Sénanque Abbey is one of the three 'Cistercian sisters of Provence'. Silvacane is the oldest by several years and Le Thoronet is plainly the most homogenous. But Sénanque in its lavender-planted valley is possibly the most appealing, particularly since it is home to a bustling monastic community. It was at the beginning of the 12th Century that a group of monks first settled at Cîteaux in Burgundy, retur-

ning to the origins of the monastic ideal – austerity, discipline, work and prayer – in reaction to the luxury that was infecting the rest of the Church. Cistercian abbeys, so-called after Cîteaux, were founded across France and Europe, based on a code of strict observance. All embellishment was banished and the decor reduced to bare necessity. The first proponents of 'form follows function' in architecture, Cistercian abbeys would remain

an influence throughout history – and some even up to the present day.
Sénanque represents a remarkable example of that uncluttered design style, stripped of all but the essentials so as to display the naked beauty of materials and spaces. The monks still work for a living, each day punctuated by services to which visitors are in some cases admitted.

W
⋀

N
⋀

N
▲

E
▲

Saint-Saturnin-les-Apt
Provence-Alpes-Côte d'Azur

The wild flora adds discrete touches of make-up. The light licks the stones and gilds the fabric of the roofs. The newly risen sun floods the plain, dispersing the smoke and giving the mists an opalescent depth. All of this perfectly evokes the Provence of our imagination. Below the ruins of this feudal chateau, Saint-Saturnin-les-Apt proudly dominates the fertile lands of Apt, its bell-tower imperiously pointed toward the sky. Noble residences testify to the

village's affluent past. The life of the village was in its surroundings: the orchards, the varied crops, the craft of pottery. Before the truffle become a rare and very expensive commodity, it grew in abundance in the surrounding oak copses and traditionally served to make a staple gruel, known locally as 'tartifle nègre' (black potato), that was eaten boiled, like potatoes. Four miles from here is Apt where candied fruit production has been a

specialty since Roman times. Bigarreau cherries, plums, melons and Provencal watermelon all go to make these succulent treats, of which 15-20,000 tons are exported every year. The Saturday morning market is another well-established tradition, known especially for its game. Customers flock here from 30 miles around for a day of pleasure in the shade of the plane trees.

S

W

S
▲

W
▲

The Verdon Gorge
Provence-Alpes-Côte d'Azur

Giono wrote: 'Nothing is more romantic than this mixture of rocks and chasms, green waters and purple shadows.'

The Verdon Gorge are a symphony of panoramic viewpoints and superlatives: 'Point Sublime' at the entrance to the main canyon; 'Corniche Sublime' that plunges to depths of 980-2,289 feet, between rocks that seem to have been split apart by some mighty axe; and 'viewpoints', one after another, along a 13-mile route where the water rushes in a torrent at a gradient of close to 15 percent in places. This is our very own Colorado – but on a French scale needless to say! The rocks are not red and the plateaus are not western deserts.

Formerly a Resistance stronghold, these rocks are home to charming little towns that nestle in the crevices – such as Moustiers-Sainte-Marie, famous for its pottery – and castles that overhang chasms.

The rapids that you can canoe down here are not as violent as their American counterparts but, being spiked with rocks and knocking your fragile craft in every direction, they are no less dangerous and do require solid experience.

Everything suddenly calms down when you reach the immense Sainte-Croix Lake, created in 1972 by the building of an EDF dam. Bauduen which once looked down on the river from a height of 3,270 feet is now more or less level with the water. Les-Salles-sur-Verdon was swallowed up altogether, a tragedy for its inhabitants despite the building of a new village.

N

E

W

N

The ochre quarries of Rustrel
Provence-Alpes-Côte d'Azur

The villages in this area are ablaze with these extraordinary massifs of pale saffron-colored brown ochre – from Rustrel (pictured here) to the glowing quarries of Roussillon or the Demoiselles Coiffées in Bédoin, at the foot of Mount Ventoux. Color is so much the mark of this environment, from its curved tiles to its plaster façades, that you could easily think you were on location for the filming of a Western. The glowing colors of Venaissin County are the hues of time immemorial, when the sea covered these lands then retreated leaving aprons of sand, clay and fine-grained iron deposits. These oxidized on contact with air, dying the sands that gradually formed a concentrated, ferruginous cuirass at the surface, several feet thick. The ore was quarried in Roussillon and here in Rustrel throughout the 19th Century, and until as recently as the 1930s.

E ⋀   S ⋀

The Calanque (creek) d'En-Vau
Provence-Alpes-Côte d'Azur
(following pages)

A fabulous site. Framed by sheer walls that look out across an immense seascape, the Calanque d'En Vau is the jewel of the coastline between Marseilles and Cassis – a place where jagged cliffs bare their soul. Below us, a steep-sided sandy cove lapped by topaz waters; a few boats anchored at the foot of limestone cliffs; and out at sea, a smattering of islands – such as the Ile Riou, only dimly visible here, a refuge for nesting seagulls. The Mediterranean in all its splendor. But enough words. Feast your eyes on this richly detailed microcosm – the Aleppo pines that punctuate the landscape, the architecture of the horizontally stratified rocks, the sheer rock faces that trap the light – streaked with colors that range from white through light gray and subtle pink to brown.

W
▲

S   W

N
⋀

E
⋀

The Mercantour Massif
Provence-Alpes-Côte d'Azur

(previous pages)

The Mercantour was once the scene of frequent confrontations between French and Italian forces fighting for control of the border. Witness the string of little redoubts, like this one on the French side. Later these became part of the famous Maginot Line in World War II. We are in the hinterland behind Nice and Menton, more than 6,540 feet up, overlooking a fabulous panorama that seems to float amid a sea of frothy clouds. The Côte d'Azur is barely 25 miles or so from here. Lower down, the Roya River flows through the eponymous valley. Lined with lovely Italian-style villages (Saorge, Breil) this was once a route for mules carrying salt to the Piedmont – an essential commodity for curing and livestock.

S
▲

W
▲

The Col (pass) de l'Izoard
Provence-Alpes-Côte d'Azur

The lunar landscapes of the Casse Déserte, on the southern flank of the Izoard Mountain (center), highlighted by thunderous clouds out toward Briançon (on the left, behind us). A host of rocky, orange peaks rises up from the rubble that fell from the ridge of the Côte Belle, at the border between the Briançon region and the *schistes lustrés* of the Italian Piedmont. The Col d'Izoard is the gateway to the Queyras region. It is also part of the legend of the Tour de France: Coppi and Bobet conquered the 7,717-foot pass three times between 1949 and 1953. On the other side, going toward Cervières in the north, the Napoleon Mountain Refuge was built with funds sent by the deposed emperor following his epic return from Elba in 1815. 'I will share my last penny with them, my last morsel of bread' he said, remembering the harshness of the climate and the warmth of his welcome by the local people.

W
⋏

N
⋏

Lake Allos
Provence-Alpes-Côte d'Azur

Suddenly, after 45 minutes' walking, a surprise. Starting out from the village resort of Allos via the little Route 226, you have taken the path that climbs through alpine pastures toward Mont Pelat – all for the sake of discovery, without knowing anything of the route except that it is long (a good four hours) but without real difficulty. This is Haute-Provence and we are already in the Alps, enjoying the combined benefits of a Mediterranean and mountain climate. Then comes the surprise: a patch of sky that has apparently tumbled between these bony, lacy, sharpened peaks and now sits glittering in the landscape like a sapphire. This radiant, azure-blue expanse is in fact Lake Allos, a perfectly natural, glacier-created marvel and the biggest lake in Europe at this altitude (7,259 feet, 50 hectares). Wandering around its waters can take hours –lingering under larches whose needles turn golden in the Fall, teasing the arctic char that breed here or simply lost in admiration amid the whistling marmots. The view from Mont Pelet, farther along, is sensational, dominating the Alpes du Sud from a height of 9,973 feet. What you will take home with you, however, is the enchanted vision of that oasis-like lake, apparently suspended in mid-air.

E

S

S
Λ

The Col de Pontis and Serre-Ponçon Lake
Provence-Alpes-Côte d'Azur

First, spend some time admiring this bejeweled landscape, set with lacy mountains topped by a fluffy ruff of clouds. Then cast your eyes across these mountain folds to the banks of the Serre-Ponçon Lake where the brightness of the freshly ploughed fields so perfectly complements the patches of lichen, russet-colored grass and leafy thorn bushes that the wild goats find so tasty. What you do not see are any human settlements, becau-se this most beautiful lake with its many creeks and inlets is in fact artificial. Its waters actually swallowed up two villages of which Savines, on the extreme right of the picture, was one.

From the Col de Pontis, a precarious spur of rock conceals the 400-foot high dam that was built in the period 1955-1960 to stabilize the flow of the River Durance, notorious for its catastrophic floods. Serre-Ponçon's huge reserve of energy is the first link in a chain of 16 hydro-electric plants that extends 156 miles to the Etang de Berre near Marseilles. In summer, the place is crowded with water sports enthusiasts and also hikers heading for the Demoiselles Coiffées Mountains, Chorges and beyond to the parks of Écrins and Queyras.

E

N

E

W

N

The Mont-Rond
Rhône-Alpes

That glittering pool of water some nine miles straight ahead is Lake Geneva. Here, in the last foothills of the Jura Mountains, the view is unrestricted by borders.

So too is the sky, billowing with masses of cottony clouds. We are in luck: cirrus and cumulus clouds combine with the soft green of the slopes to create a heavenly landscape of power and tenderness. The view from the La Faucille pass is already fantastic

– overlooking the farms scattered in the Valsérine Valley – and it remains that way slightly higher up, at the Petit Mont-Rond, an easy 45 minutes' walk from the Mont-Rond, where this photo was shot. Slightly farther up still is the serene 5,523-foot Colomby de Gex. These peaceful, undulating slopes dominate the Gex region, famous for its thermal baths and stylish casino at Divonne-les-Bains, and also for its historical connection with Voltaire:

in 1760 he settled in the hamlet of Ferney and by dint of wit and money eventually turned it into a lively town.

The proximity of Geneva and the CERN has been an additional boost to the economy in the past 25 years. Renamed the European Laboratory for Particle Physics, the CERN employs more than half of the local population and makes the Gex an unusually prosperous French region.

Lake Geneva

S

S

W

Annecy
Rhône-Alpes

View from the cobbled walkway overlooking the emerald waters of the River Thiou, with the Palais de L'Isle apparently sailing toward us like some huge stone vessel. And beyond these flowered embankments, one of the most colorful parts of Annecy Old Town. But this pristine décor is a far cry from the days when this spillway into the great lake served as the city's main thoroughfare. There were no embankments then, just a constant stream of boats bringing crops from Talloires, meat, fruit and vegetables, wheat for milling in the water mills and fish that were heaped into the pools at the foot of houses on stilts.

On the right of the picture – and therefore behind us – the striking, baroque façade of the first monastery of the Visitation, a religious order of nuns founded in the early 17th Century by local man François de Sales.

N
Λ

E
Λ

The Mont Blanc
seen from the Petit Flambeau
Rhône-Alpes
(following pages)

The Petit Flambeau is the center point of the Mont Blanc Massif from where the view sweeps over myriad peaks. This pristine solitude, alas, also conjures up other images – hellish images of the tragic accident of March 24 1999. At 10.46 that morning, some 9,800 feet directly below the person in red, a truck caught fire near the middle of the Chamonix to Courmayeur tunnel. The driver panicked and fled, forgetting that his truck was blocking 24 other heavy-duty trucks most of which also caught fire. Moments later, 39 people had either burnt or suffocated to death. A court-case ensued. The Chamonix Valley, at the heart of the European Alps, is the first to suffer from a particular form of plague: roads carved out of mountainsides that attract chaotic convoys of air-polluting trucks.

E
▲

E
⋏

S
⋏

The Mont Blanc Summit
Rhône-Alpes
(previous pages)

Franck Charel dreamed of this moment. Photographing the summit of the Mont Blanc, preferably when the glaciers and peaks are tinged with pink by the early morning sun. This photo was taken at 9.30 am, with the clouds just beginning to cluster around the medium-height peaks. Shooting from 15,700 feet, Franck pans from left to right, moving from the snow blown by a 25 mph wind to the peaks themselves: the Arête des Bosses, the Désert de Platé, the Aiguilles Rouges, the Aiguille du Midi, the Mont Maudit, the Mont Blanc du Tacul, The Dent du Géant, the Grandes Jorasses and the Mont Buet. It was from this last mountain – known to machos as 'the woman's Mont Blanc' - that the wives of pioneering climbers would peer through their binoculars at their intrepid husbands. These days, in fine weather, it's not unusual to find 200 people trampling the snows here on the roof of Europe.

W ⏶

N ⏶

The Massif de La Chartreuse
seen from the Charmant Som
Rhône-Alpes

This massif, between Grenoble and Chambéry, is a perfect natural stronghold. Its impenetrable, sheer limestone walls are clearly visible all along the A41 freeway – also in this dreamy picture, taken from the Charmont Som.

The Gorges du Guiers is one of the few canyons (and valleys) that actually lead into the Massif de la Chartreuse. Flanked by steep-sided cliffs, the gorge lies at the foot of the Grande Chartreuse that nestles in the cirque just visible here, despite the shadows, on the right. The Grand Chartreuse is the headquarters of the Carthusian order founded by St. Bruno in 1084 and based, then as now, on meditation punctuated by intellectual and manual activity. There are currently 24 charterhouses located around the globe, including more recently in the USA.

E
▲

S
▲

Mont Blanc Massif

The Désert de Platé
Rhône-Alpes

A desert, no less, at an altitude of some 8,000 feet. Directly ahead of us is the Mont Blanc, clearly visible some 12 miles away. Also the Giffre Mountains.

Truth is, this high plateau is not as deserted as it seems. All year round, wild goats are willing subjects to be photographed like movie stars by tourists who can easily get here via the cable car. They call it progress. The Platé is a 25-mile square area of entirely denuded, treacherous terrain, at an altitude of 5,232-8,175 feet. Its surface is fissured with chasms that form a network of branches within the rock, maintained by melting snow and run-off. Experts have a fairly simple explanation for these gaping fissures that can engulf reckless hikers: carbon-dioxide in the water dissolves the limestone at the surface, creating rivulets (known locally as 'lapiaz') that join up with the underground network referred to above. The Platé is part of the Sixt nature reserve, close to the Dents Blanches on the Swiss border. Taken as a whole, the Sixt represents a remarkable mountainous expanse that extends over more than 9,000 hectares and includes the Lac du Vogealle.

The only problem, as is so often the case these days, is the clash between ecology and economy. Plans are now partly on hold for the development of the ski station at the lovely village of Sixt, clustered around its lime tree at the mouth of the great Fer à Chevel cirque. Everyone hopes that what now seems an obstacle will gradually come to be seen as a blessing in disguise.

W

N

W
▲

N
▲

The Col du Galibier
Rhône-Alpes

Straddling Savoie and the Dauphiné, the Col du Galibier is part of the legend of the Tour de France that since 1911 has included this grand and austere high-mountain pass among its climbs.

Enthusiasts will recall the battle between Pantani and Ullrich in 1998, fought out along the twists and turns of the north slope, the steepest and roughest section coming from Maurienne, with the real challenges starting at Plan-Lachat. Here, looking out toward the peaks of Les Trois Evêchés and Le Grand Calibier that frame the main pass (8,649 feet), one recalls that until 1860 the Col du Galibier marked the frontier between France and Italy. Three years earlier, Victor-Emmanuel and Napoleon III struck an agreement to build a railway tunnel more than eight miles long through the Alps. It was a colossal construction project, working more or less simultaneously from Bardonecchia at one end and Modane nearly 19 miles to the east as the crow flies. This was the first use of the revolutionary compressed-air tools invented by engineer Germain Sommellier. Hammering at a rate of 180 strokes per minute, they dug more than six feet of tunnel every day and joined up the two ends in September 1870. The entrance at the Modane end is now a listed historical monument.

E

S

W
▲

N
▲

Lake Blanc
Rhône-Alpes

This is the view you get at an altitude of 7,848 feet, 2,289 feet above the top of the Lake Blanc cable car – a fabulous panoramic view of the Mont Blanc Massif's most beautiful summits.

Winter and summer alike, whether you are travelling on foot or on skis, Lake Blanc – which is green – then Lakes Milieu and Fare, all link up with this fabulous string of peaks, ridges, caps and legendary needles that you see before you. On the left, the Aiguille d'Argentiere, with the glacier of the same name immediately below it; in the middle, the Aiguille Verte and Les Drus; and on the right the Grandes Jorasses, the Aiguille de Chamonix and the Mont Blanc. Summits one has dreamed of since childhood, immortalized by the writer Frison-Roche. Few places can boast such a panorama of peaks.

L'Aiguille Verte Mt   Les Drus Massif

S

E ⛰

Grandes Jorasses Mt   Dent du Géant Mt

S ⛰

The Aiguille du Midi
Rhône-Alpes

The cable car from Chamonix whisks you to the Aiguille du Midi in just 20 minutes, plunging you into the heart of the extraordinary Mont Blanc Massif. It is as if you had been spirited by magic from planet Earth to this heady, rooftop world studded with snow-capped peaks. The journey is in two stages, stopping midway at the 7,576-foot Plan de l'Aiguille before climbing the remaining 4,900 feet to the Aiguille du Midi. This second stage is a real tour de force considering the complete absence of pylons. The cable cars and their air-borne passengers are suspended from a 45-ton cable that is held tight by a 50-ton counterweight mechanism spread between four wells more than 80 feet deep within the Plan de l'Aiguille. More than half a century after it was first opened, Italian engineer Vittorio Zignoli's technological – and ecological – achievement remains a thing of wonder.

W
⋏

N
⋏

Palombaggia Beach
Corsica
(following pages)

Silence. A herd of elephants lies asleep in the peaceful evening light. Near a teetering stone slab, a gigantic boiled egg awaits a gargantuan appetite. Beyond it, a parasol pine echoes the curves of the hills. This bizarre but beautiful marine jungle is Palombaggia in the gulf of Porto-Vecchio – a name that melts in the mouth.
Framed by russet rocks, Palombaggia beach looks out toward the Cerbicale Archipelago. Its long strip of white sand is one of the wonders of nature, much sought after by sun lovers who either find it by accident or through travel agencies – who knows. Secretly, of course, all of us at some time or another could be seduced by such solitude, such untrammeled beauty...
To see Palombaggia is to cherish the memory forever.

E
▲

S
▲

The Lavezzi Islands
Corsica
(previous pages)

This emerald green jewel of a coast, just a few miles off Cape Pertusato at the southern tip of Corsica, is a major conservation area. Just as well really, when Cavallo Island, slightly farther north and the biggest island in the Lavezzi Archipelago, is now the exclusive property of 'millionaire owners' whose dream homes are protected by heavily armed guards. The archipelago as a whole is in fact a classified nature reserve, being home to an abundance of marine flora that is faced with extinction elsewhere. Geologists regard this archipelago and the string of little islands that separate Corsica from nearby Sardinia as evidence that the two islands were originally joined. The legacy is a channel strewn with reefs and especially hazardous due to the appalling violence of the Mediterranean's mysterious winds. Witness the number of ships that have finished up on the rocks.

W ▲

N ▲

Tino Rossi Harbor, Ajaccio
Corsica

It was inevitable that Corsica should pay tribute to the singer who made her famous throughout the world: Tino Rossi (1907-1983) dubbed the 'emperor of romance', the 'Napoleon of records'. The old harbor in Ajaccio at the foot of the citadel was accordingly renamed the Port Tino Rossi. You are lucky – or privileged – to find a mooring for your boat here in summer. Space is all the more limited because this exquisite site is a great place to watch life in old Ajaccio. The palms and plane trees of the nearby Place du Maréchal-Foch provide cooling shade in summer. Some 50 yards away, the air is filled with the smell of onion and Mediterranean herbs from the morning market, bustling with lovers of 'coppa' and 'lonzu'. In the vaulted canteens next door, thirsty customers order the 'little wines' of Sartène or a Coteaux d'Ajaccio. Immediately behind is the busy Rue Fesch and the little streets of the old quarter – with the sea view always seductive.

N

The Ile Rousse
Corsica

Pietra is a small island linked to terra firma by a jetty (pictured here). The view from the lighthouse over this fiercely jagged red granite coastline is unique. The military and commercial harbor on Isula Rossa ('red island') dates from the 18th Century, built by nationalist hero Pasquale Paoli to compete with Genovese domination on nearby Calvi and Algajola. These days, the Ile Rousse and surrounding area are packed with thousands of holidaymakers who come here for the white beaches of ultra-fine sand and the superb scenery, dominated by some of the loveliest terraced villages in Corsica – villages like Sant'Antonino, Cateri, Speloncato, Belgodère and others like it, criss-crossed with cobbled, stepped lanes and vaulted passageways leading to small squares that look out to sea. Aregno and Ville-di-Paraso in the Balagne region, with their orchards, recall the area's former prosperity when every village would have pressed its olives in its own mills and exported its oranges and figs. The Balagne countryside today lies fallow, devastated by war, the collapse of the rural economy and repeated fires. Tourism and artistic craftwork – much of it excellent, as in Pigna – now shape a different kind of life. We might almost say, a different Corsica.

S   W
▲   ▲

E
▲

S
▲

Erbalunga
Corsica

Cape Corse has never recovered from the terrible bloodletting of the First World War. Despite the extraordinary courage of its womenfolk, this landscape of terraced escarpments, so meticulously cultivated over the centuries, has never been the same since. That's just how it is. Witness what you see around you. The mountain directly ahead of us that points into the Mediterranean like a finger of God once bore on its flanks an abundance of gardens, orchards and lush terraces planted with cereal crops and vegetables - an agricultural and pastoral economy which, supported by fishing, guaranteed a day-to-day living that was good enough – not luxurious but never poor. Most of the patiently constructed little walls are now crumbling but, given the extent of neglect, it is now too late to restore plots of land perched between sky and land – not to grow crops that cost less at the supermarket ...

Erbalunga, to the north of Bastia, is one of the ports fortified by the Genoese in the 16th Century, at the expense of the inhabitants. That round tower sits on a base several yards thick. From the upper level – these days most often roofless, as here – lookouts would keep watch for unexpected ships, quickly alerting the entire island thanks to a network of watchtowers that still punctuate the Corsican coast. In the background, the houses bathe in water.

W

N

Acknowledgements

I would like to thank all the people who have made this book possible:

Flo, my parents, my sister and my family who supported me.

Profound thanks to Yann and Anne Arthus-Bertrand, Françoise Leroch', Hélène de Bonis, Isabelle Lechenet, Erwan Sourget, Françoise Jacquot, Philippe Bourseiller, Jacques Barthélémy, my photographic family from whom I have learned so much.

My friend Jean-Michel Delavaud, director of Agence Jade Communication, who believed in me from the start. Thanks too to Annette Bowden.

Fujifilm France. Thanks to Bruno Baudry, Marc Héraud and Édith Coiquaud for their support.

Cécile Dourmap, Emmanuel Achin, Frédéric Gueguen, Maryse Chaboisseau, Richard Hay and Stéphane Cutxan at Dahinden Janjac who took such good care of my films.

Thanks to everyone in the Vigie Graphique team, Éric Massé, Larissa Bohême, Maryse Trépy, Thierry Vançon and Fabrice Borio.

Jean-Hervé Sévézen and everyone in the Zedrimtim team (www.zedrimtim.com) for creating and maintaining my internet site.

Franck Bigot and everyone at Agence H2O

(www.h2o-communication.com).
Thanks to Werner and Peter Seitz for their trust in me, and likewise to Urs Krebs at the Swiss company Seitz Phototechnik.
All of the photos in this book were taken with a Roundshot 220 (www.roundshot.ch)

Gilles Quinqueneau from Shop photo Canon Prony.

Huge thanks to Jacques Barthélémy who gave me permission to take the photo at the summit of Mont-Blanc, and likewise to Alain Payot, Frédéric Ancey and Véronique Périllat.

Thanks to Stéphanie Paolini for the wise advice of a mountain-loving doctor..

Isabelle Jendron and Philippe Pierrelée from Éditions du Chêne, and likewise Valérie Tognali for her editorial supervision.

Jean Taverne for agreeing to place his writing alongside my photos.

And thanks to all of those near and far who have played a part in this project:

Monique Labadie, Bernard Dectot, Jean-François Bardy, Éric Colmet Daage, Agnès Grégoire, Sylvie Rebbot, Jean-Luc Marty, Joan le Boru, Daniel Yonnet, Pierre Pinelli, Jean-Paul Ayme, Juliette Pascal, Bruno Morini, Dominique Carrier, Cyril Drouhet, Wanda Schmollgruber, Jean-Marie Montali, Arnaud Frich, Joël Halioua, Marie-Françoise and Albert Paolini, Marie-France and Claude Charpentier, Chantal and Stéphane Mougel, Masako Sakata, Emmanuel Nunès, François Xavier Mazurier, Lisa and Laurent Frérebaut, Jean-Bernard Cloet, Delphine and Sylvain Mercier, Hervé Rossi, Marie-Pierre Vuitton, Cécile Caillaud, Pierre-André Chalamel, Teo Vriboligi, Danielle Lecouturier, Jacques Bigot, Elsa Berlanger, Christophe Serrano, Denis Cuisy, Arlette and Gérard Loshouarn, Gaëlle Bailly.

All of the photos in this book were shot in medium format on Fujichrome Velvia film.

You will find my photos on the website www.franckcharel.com

The photo of the Mont Blanc massif seen from the Petit Flambeau was taken on 11 September 2001. I would like to dedicate this photo to the New Yorkers who disappeared on that day.

Metro Books
122 Fifth Avenue
New York, NY 10011

ISBN-13: 978-1-4351-0473-0
ISBN-10: 1-4351-0473-0

Printed and bound in China by Midas Printing Ltd.

1 3 5 7 9 10 8 6 4 2

Where the photos were taken

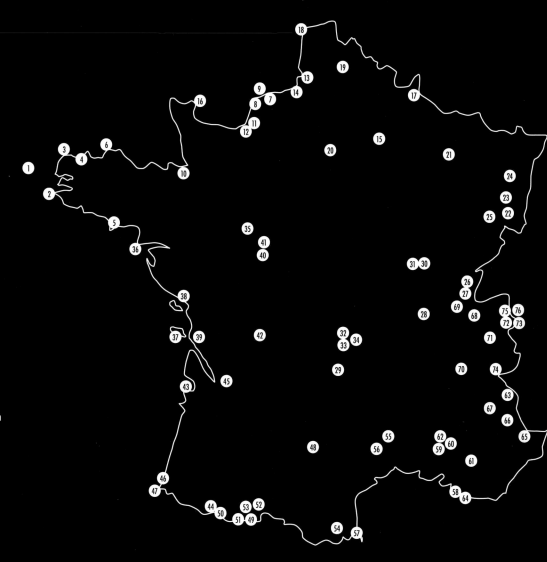
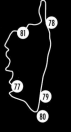